MW01680944

A Quake To Remember

by Meish Goldish
illustrated by Wayne Hovis

Harcourt
SCHOOL PUBLISHERS

Printed in the United States of America

ISBN 10: 0-15-351109-5
ISBN 13: 978-0-15-351109-7

Ordering Options
ISBN 10: 0-15-350603-2 (Grade 6 On-Level Collection)
ISBN 13: 978-0-15-350603-1 (Grade 6 On-Level Collection)
ISBN 10: 0-15-357987-0 (package of 5)
ISBN 13: 978-0-15-357987-5 (package of 5)

1 2 3 4 5 6 7 8 9 10 179 12 11 10 09 08 07 06

Sarah sat in a chair, deep in thought. Grandpa entered the room. "What are you thinking about?" he asked.

"I've got a school report to do," she replied. "It's about the San Francisco earthquake of 1906."

Grandpa looked thoughtful . "Oh, that was the big one," he said. "I know all about it."

Sarah looked puzzled. "You do?" she asked. "How could that be, Grandpa? Wasn't that many years before you were born?"

"That's correct," Grandpa said, "but I heard many stories about the great quake from my mother. That's your great-grandmother, the one we call GG."

Sarah's eyes widened. "Oh, Grandpa, please tell me what GG told you," she exclaimed. "I could use the information in my report. It would make it so interesting!"

Grandpa sat on the sofa and relaxed. "Well, it all began on the morning of April 18th," he said. "GG always remembered that because it was her birthday."

"How old was she in 1906?" Sarah asked.

"Let's see," Grandpa said, adding numbers in his head. "That year, GG turned eleven, the same age that you are now. How about that!"

Sarah smiled.

"The quake struck early in the morning," Grandpa continued, "just a little after five o'clock. GG said it woke her with a shock. She felt like she was rolling on ocean waves. Her bed glided across the room. The whole thing made her very disoriented. It took her a few seconds to figure out what was happening."

"What did she do?" Sarah asked.

"She raced out of her house with her parents," Grandpa replied. "They were still in their pajamas and slippers. They didn't even have time to put on their shoes."

"Why not?" Sarah asked.

"Because everything was crashing around them," Grandpa explained. "Picture this in your mind: Dishes and books were haphazardly flying off shelves and falling to the floor. Pictures on the walls came crashing to the ground. Windows broke, and even parts of the ceiling caved in. Everyone was too scared to stay inside the house another second!"

Sarah closed her eyes and tried to imagine the scene. "That's terrible," she gasped.

"They were lucky to get out of their home alive," Grandpa said. "Some people weren't as fortunate. However, things weren't much better out in the streets."

"What do you mean?" Sarah asked.

Grandpa shook his head. "GG told me it was unbelievable," he recalled. "The shaking of the ground caused buildings to collapse. The roads were paved with bricks, and they just ripped apart. There was an animal stable near GG's home. She saw lots of horses running loose in the streets."

"It sounds like a movie," Sarah gasped.

"Only this was real," Grandpa replied. "Do you know the train cars that we ride here in the streets?"

"You mean the trolley cars?" Sarah asked.

"Yes," said Grandpa. "Well, San Francisco had them back in 1906, too. Those cars fell over on their sides like toys. The tracks came loose and twisted like pretzels."

"How long did the earthquake last?" Sarah asked.

"The earthquake lasted only about a minute," Grandpa said. "That wasn't the end of it, though. GG told me that fires soon broke out all over the city. That's because gas lines under the ground were torn apart. Electric wires came loose from street poles. When the electric sparks met the gas in the air, BOOM! Suddenly, another fire had broken out. Pretty soon much of the city was burning."

"What did GG do?" Sarah asked.

"It was imperative that she and her parents find a safe place to go. They followed thousands of people who walked to San Francisco Bay. They hoped to get on a ferry boat to Oakland, the city on the other side of the bay."

"Did they make it?" Sarah asked.

"They got to the bay," Grandpa said, "but thousands of people were rushing to the few boats that were available. GG told me that too many people were trying to get on each ferry. She feared the boats might capsize in the water."

Sarah could hardly wait to hear more. "What did she do next?" she asked.

Grandpa sighed, "GG and her parents left and walked all the way from the bay to Golden Gate Park."

"Was it safe there?" Sarah asked.

"It was safer than many other places in the city," Grandpa replied. "That's because the park is on higher ground, so the fires couldn't spread there as quickly."

Now Grandpa began to laugh. "What's so funny?" Sarah asked.

Grandpa explained, "I was just remembering how GG described the scene. She said people were carrying all their belongings to the park. They held boxes and trunks filled with clothes and food. One woman held a birdcage with four kittens inside it. The bird sat on her arm. I always laugh when I think about that. It must have looked so odd!"

"Did the fire department put out all of the fires?" Sarah asked.

Grandpa shook his head. "They couldn't," he said. "The earthquake had torn apart most of the city's water pipes. The fire hydrants were broken, so firefighters couldn't connect their hoses. They filled buckets of water from the bay, but it wasn't enough to do much good."

"Did the fires keep spreading?" Sarah asked.

"Oh, yes," Grandpa replied, "for three days. The flames spread to thousands of homes and office buildings and never receded."

Sarah was curious. "Did GG's house burn down?" she asked.

Grandpa said, "Actually, it was blown up by the fire department. They did it on purpose. Since they couldn't put out the flames with water, the firefighters decided to dynamite all the homes and buildings in its path. They wanted to starve the fire. They hoped the fire would go out if there was nothing new to burn."

Sarah's mouth opened in amazement. "Lots of people must have lost their homes," she gasped.

"You're right," Grandpa agreed. "About 250,000 people became homeless. Some homes were destroyed completely. Others needed a lot of repairs before people could move back in."

"Where did the people go?" Sarah asked.

"They lived outdoors," Grandpa said. "The city set up thousands of tents in parks. That's where GG and her parents ended up for some time. GG said it was very hard living there, but she tried to stay optimistic."

"How did they get food?" Sarah asked.

"The city set up food stations," Grandpa said, "but GG told me she and her parents had to wait in line for hours to get something to eat. She said the lines were five blocks long!"

"Was there any water to drink?" Sarah asked.

"All the water had to be shipped in from other towns," Grandpa replied.

"What about clothing?" Sarah asked.

"The city supplied that, too," Grandpa explained. "Once word of the earthquake spread, lots of people from other states sent clothes and blankets to the homeless here. GG once showed me a blanket she got from someone back then. She was very grateful for it and never threw it away."

Sarah was curious. "Did the fires ever reach the park?" she asked.

"Thankfully, no," Grandpa said. "However, they did keep on burning in the city for three days. About five hundred city blocks burned to the ground before the fires finally stopped."

Sarah seemed both surprised and puzzled. "How were the fires finally put out?" she asked. "I thought you said there wasn't any water."

Grandpa replied, "That's right, there wasn't any water. It was the wind that did the job."

"What do you mean?" Sarah asked.

"During the first three days after the quake, the wind blew toward the city," Grandpa explained. "That helped to spread the flames. However, after three days, the wind shifted direction. It blew the flames toward the bay instead of the city. By then, there was almost nothing left to burn. Three-fourths of San Francisco was in ashes!"

Sarah could barely speak. "Wow," she gasped. She paused and finally asked, "How long did GG and her parents live in a tent?"

"They stayed there for about two months," Grandpa replied. "Then the city built them a green wooden shack. GG once gave me a picture of it. Wait here. I think I still have it."

Grandpa went to his room. A minute later, he returned with a photo. He pointed to a girl and two adults in the picture. "That's GG and your great-great grandparents," he said proudly.

Sarah's eyes widened. "Wow!" she exclaimed. "GG looks a lot like me!"

Grandpa smiled. "I think so, too," he said. "She was also optimistic, just like you. Lots of people were unhappy and full of remorse. They feared that San Francisco would never get back to normal, but they were wrong. GG told me they were delivering mail to people in tents just a few days after the quake. How's that for service!"

Grandpa saw that Sarah was deep in thought. "What are you thinking now?" he asked.

Sarah said, "I'm thinking how grateful I should be for what I have. I know I complain about things, but now I see how lucky I really am."

Grandpa smiled. "Now you even sound like your great-grandmother," he said. "GG would have told you to be grateful for each day. After all, no one had a premonition about what would happen on that day in 1906. We never know exactly what may happen tomorrow. All we can do is take life as it comes."

"Just stay optimistic," Sarah added.

"That's right," Grandpa said, hugging her tightly. "Stay optimistic!"

Think Critically

1. How could you tell that Sarah was eager to learn about the earthquake?
2. What caused fires to break out in the city after the earthquake hit?
3. Why do you think GG always kept the blanket she was given after the quake?
4. What important lesson about life can you learn from the story?
5. Would you have remained in San Francisco after living through the earthquake of 1906? Explain.

Science

More on Earthquakes Do research on how earthquakes occur. Find out which areas in the United States are most prone to earthquakes. Design a poster to share your information.

School-Home Connection Share with your family the story that Grandpa shared with Sarah. Imagine you could each save only one item from your home when escaping a quake. Let each family member tell what item he or she would choose, and why.

Word Count: 1,603